HOW TO TAKE CHARGE OF YOUR LIFE

by Mildred Newman and
Bernard Berkowitz
Authors of the super-selling
HOW TO BE YOUR OWN BEST FRIEND

"With the help of this penetrating book you will dare to discover more about who you really are. And you'll find comfort and challenge and wisdom to take with you on your journey toward becoming your own finest self."

—Dr. Elizabeth Thorne
President, National Association
for Psychoanalysis

"*How to Take Charge of Your Life* gives you guides to defining and becoming the kind of person you want to be."

—*San Diego Union*

HOW TO
TAKE CHARGE OF
YOUR LIFE

By Mildred Newman
and Bernard Berkowitz

BANTAM BOOKS
TORONTO · NEW YORK · LONDON · SYDNEY

*This low-priced Bantam Book
has been completely reset in a type face
designed for easy reading, and was printed
from new plates. It contains the complete
text of the original hard-cover edition.*
NOT ONE WORD HAS BEEN OMITTED.

HOW TO TAKE CHARGE OF YOUR LIFE
A Bantam Book

PRINTING HISTORY

Harcourt Brace Jovanovich edition published May 1977
2nd printing .... *May 1977*
A selection of the PSYCHOLOGY TODAY *Book Club/October 1977*

Bantam edition / May 1978
2nd printing .... *May 1978*   4th printing .... *July 1980*
3rd printing ...... *October 1979*   5th pritinng .... *July 1981*

ISBN 0-553-20343-6

Published simultaneously in the United States and Canada

PRINTED IN THE UNITED STATES OF AMERICA

14 13 12 11 10 9

Dedicated to

Dr. Ruth Pirkle Berkeley

A woman we admire

CONTENTS

ONE

Would You Believe?

Two thousand five hundred years ago Aesop told this story:

It was a bright sunny morning in a mountain village. An old man and his grandson were going to the market in the large town in the valley to sell a donkey. The donkey was beautifully groomed and brushed and they set off happily down the steep path. In a while they passed some people lounging by the side of the path.

"Look at that silly pair," said one of the onlookers. "There they go, scrambling and stumbling down the path, when they could be riding comfortably on the back of that sure-footed beast."

The old man heard this and thought it was right. So he and the boy mounted the donkey and thus they continued their descent.

3

Soon they passed another group of people gossiping by the wayside.

"Look at the lazy pair—breaking the back of that poor donkey."

The old man thought they were right and since he was the heavier, he decided to walk while the boy rode.

In a little while they heard more comments.

"Look at that disrespectful child—he rides while the old man walks."

The old man thought they were right, and it was only proper that he should ride while the boy walked.

Sure enough, they soon heard this:

"What a mean old man riding at his ease while the poor child has to try to keep up on foot."

By this time the old man and the boy were becoming increasingly bewildered. When they finally overheard the criticism that the donkey would be all worn out and no one would want to buy him after the long walk to the market, they sat down, dejected, by the side of the road.

After the donkey had been allowed to rest for a while, they continued the journey, but in a completely different manner.

Thus it was, late that afternoon, that the old man

and the boy were seen gasping breathlessly into the marketplace. Slung on a pole between them, hung by his tied feet, was the donkey!

As Aesop said:

"You can't please everyone."

If you try, you lose yourself.

———•———

Two thousand years ago a great teacher named Hillel wrote a little poem that rhymes in Aramaic.

"If I'm not for myself,
Then who can be for me?
And if I'm only for myself,
Then what am I?
And if not now,
When?"

About seven hundred years ago another teacher named Sosya, ripe with years and honors, lay dying. His students and disciples asked if he was afraid to die.

"Yes," he said. "I'm afraid to meet my Maker."

"How can that be? You have lived such an exemplary life. You have led us out of the wilderness of ignorance, like Moses."

"You have judged between us wisely, like Solomon."

Sosya replied: "When I meet my Maker, He will not ask, 'Have you been Moses or Solomon?'

"He will ask, 'Have you been Sosya?!' "

————•————

Being your own person . . .

A modern problem?

Not on your life.

We have chosen just a few examples from times past. There are many more, equally good.

Examples of what?

That in every age people have had to struggle to be themselves,

to use their own heads,

to run their own show,

to take charge of their own lives.

What do we have to add to the thinking on this age-old problem?

Insight.

What's that?

The hidden payoff.

The secret satisfaction. What you get from *not* being in charge of your life.

What kind of secret satisfaction could there possibly be in feeling pushed around?

What's so wonderful about feeling trapped, chained, coerced?

How can anyone possibly get any joy out of feeling weak, impotent, victimized?

Would you believe
If you play it weak and meek,
You think they're sure to love you?

Would you believe
If you seem to be going along with the crowd,
You feel protected from blame?

Would you believe
If you keep both hands tied behind you,
Then you expect someone to feed you?

Would you believe
That in your helpless state

You secretly believe you are controlling the whole world?

Would you believe
That by limping through life
You feel you are rewriting your past?

Would you believe
That by never being able to make up your mind
Everything is possible?

Would you believe
That when you stab yourself
"They" bleed?

Would you believe
That when you fall on your face
"They" 'll be sorry?

You had better believe it—and more!

No amount of determination, no amount of will power, of inspiration or exhortation is enough as long as you are in the dark about your own secret payoff.

NO DECISION IS A DECISION TOO!

No decision is a decision, too!

The hidden goal in being indecisive, in not taking charge of your life is: to hold on to your mother and father—forever.

Decisions were their job when you were little.

Being in charge of you—that's what they did.

Your mother or your father told you what to do.

Maybe now you ask your uncle or your best friend, or your friendly doctor, or your bartender, to make the tough decisions for you.

But it's all the same thing.

For you to take over is to give up your parents and lose that connection with them.

And to feel all alone.

Sometimes there's no problem in knowing which decision to make. You know you have to go to the dentist. You know you have to go to the dry cleaners. And you keep putting it off, and you nag yourself about it, and you make yourself solemn promises to pick up the phone and make that appointment. But you always think about it . . .

When you're in the shower or riding a bus, so you can have more promises and some more recriminations.

"Why do I do that?" you ask yourself.

"I know what I have to do, why don't I just *do* it?"

Would you believe
It keeps you company?
If you listen to that inner nagging voice, does it sound like
your mother?
your father?
Grandma?
Grandpa?
Uncle John?
Aunt Marie?
That's a lot to give up and you run the risk of feeling lonely.

The moment *you* decide is the moment when you really leave home.

Now you're on your own, for the first time in your life.

It's new, strange, and unfamiliar.

Think that is an exaggeration?

A man in his thirties, when he first recognized how he had been carrying his mother around with him all his life, was shaken to the very bottom of his sense of self and moaned: "Who will I be without her inside me, telling me what to do?

"Who will tell me what to do now?"

If you are in charge of your life, does it mean you give up the feeling of being taken care of? Not at all—as an adult you give and you also get.

If you are in charge of your life, does it mean no one will love you? Not at all—you'll be loved all the more.

If you can do it for yourself, does it mean no one will ever want to do it for you? Remember, after a certain time in your life *whatever* gets done is up to you.

If you act for yourself, does it mean no one will ever take pity on you and help you? Why get help that way? That's no way to feel good about yourself.

If you do things your way and not "theirs," does it mean you can be blamed if things go wrong? Yes, you may make some wrong decisions, but they'll be *your* decisions and you'll also get the credit for the right ones. No one is perfect.

It's safer to be passive, childish, always waiting for the cue from others, but then you have become a shadow. "They" can't get angry if you follow "their" lead, but then you wonder why you cannot call your life your own.

**MAKING A DECISION REVEALS
SOMETHING ABOUT YOU**

Making a decision is telling people who you are. Then they'll find out all your secrets.

If your purpose in life is not to reveal who you are, the best thing for you is to remain indecisive.

Do you need to present the image of a harmless nobody so that you are not suspected of harboring secret ambitions? If you do, then don't make decisions.

Do you secretly believe that everything and anything is possible for you? Then by all means don't have a decisive thought, don't lift a finger in your own behalf. It is only possible to be anything and to have anything if you are willing to give up all the other possibilities.

For example, if you decide to take a vacation in Florida, that means you have given up California.

To choose one goal means to give up others.

If you affirm yourself in a certain way, that means that you are turning your back on all other ways of being.

It means you can't have everything.
It means you can't do everything.
It means you can't be everything.

It means you can't please everybody.

———————•———————

If you avoid decisions, you never have to face the harsh reality that you can't be in two places at the same time.

And nobody can make you accept it.

So that makes indecisive you bigger and more powerful than everybody.

You are surrounded by life's attractions and don't know which way to turn.

But no one can make you choose.

Not choosing is exhausting.

The dread of missing out on something out there leads you to pass up something here.

Going around in circles takes energy that you would otherwise have available to you, if you had made a decision, *any decision*.

But the effort to keep yourself anchored in dead center may be worth it.

If you strike out in a definite direction, you are giving up dreams of infinite possibilites.

When you make a choice, you may be running the risk of rejecting the values of certain people.

They may be able to see that you are really not the way they would want you to be—not like them.

So by sitting tight, you may be able to retain the love and approval of different people whose values may contradict each other.

Your indecisiveness helps you to avoid trying to reconcile the irreconcilables.

Try to be all things to all people and *you* disappear.

What if everyone loves you but your sense of self is lost?

TWO

Leaving Home Is *Not* Enough

Being in charge of your own life is growing up.

Being your own person means being on your own.

It's a great feeling, but a little scary.

It may seem once you've left home that you are your own person.

But *being in charge of your life* not only means getting away, leaving your family—*it also means putting your family outside of yourself.*

Putting your family outside of yourself?

Strange idea.

How do you know you're carrying them around inside you?

It's like: You are about to fall asleep and you remember you haven't brushed your teeth. You feel so sleepy, you don't want to get up, but you know you should. You hassle yourself this way most every night. If you listen to the voices in the argument going on inside you, whose voice do you hear?

It's like: "They" want you to call home "regularly" and you resist it. "Why should I?" you think. But you also think, "I should." You spend a lot of time, maybe more than you realize, resenting and not calling and feeling "funny" about it.

It's like: You're getting things done, doing your job, but it feels like an uphill fight. It is as if there is somebody there criticizing you, making fun of you. You feel the constant need to justify what you do, to prove you have a right to do it, to do it your way.

It's like: Whenever you get to know someone who might really be the "right" person for you, you suddenly lose interest. Why? Do you secretly think of all the things that "they" might say about that person?

It's like: You feel you're being followed. You know it's not true, but there is a kind of feeling "they" are after you, "they" will catch you—that you'll "get it."

It's like: You're feeling pretty good about yourself, and what you're doing. But no one seems to appreciate it. Nobody thinks it's a big deal. "They" haven't noticed. And it turns into nothing for you. You feel hopeless and useless.

If you have any feelings like these, then it may be that "they" are shadowy presences weighing you down.

You can get rid of them if you recognize them for what they are.

They are your parents (or whoever raised you).

They are your family and you haven't quite shaken yourself loose.

How do you shake yourself loose?

It's not enough to leave physically—you can be thousands of miles away and still hear their voices.

On the other hand, you can be living in the same house and still be your own person.

The emotional separation does not mean a lack of feeling. It does not mean being cold and distant.

It *does* mean: You are you, and they are who they are.

And it doesn't mean that they are unfair if they don't see life the way you do.

Nor does it mean that you are a terrible person if you don't see life the way they do.

It simply means: *You haven't given yourself the right to be different.*

You insist that they have to change and tell you that you are right.

If you really know it for yourself, you don't have to hear it from them.

Don't be such a tyrant.

Give them the same right to their views that you would like for yourself.

When you were young and trying to understand what other people were like inside, it was natural for you to assume that they were the same as you were; that they had the same feelings you did.

This is not always the case.

To be separate is to accept and recognize that there is a difference.

It is only through the acceptance and recognition that you are you, and not like anybody else, that you can become your own person and have your very own life.

It is a tricky concept, but any child can understand it. Do you remember when you felt that if you closed your eyes, the world disappeared?

Do you remember your dad being oh-so-proud, and feeling good about himself, because of something you did or said?

Do you remember your mother telling you that if you misbehaved you made her unhappy, and if you got sick she would be upset?

So her happiness depended on you.

Her feelings were inside you.

You controlled them, and since you cared about how she felt, you were controlled by them.

And so, you could still be believing that if you cut yourself—she would bleed.

And if it were more important to you to make her bleed than anything else, you would give up your whole life, you would give up your separate self to keep that connection. When you keep those others inside you, your life is preoccupied with making space for them.

You spend so much energy taking care of the family inside you.

You have so little left over for yourself.

With your parents inside you, you are already giving them so much—giving them a free ride—that you have no energy left to give them something in reality.

When they expect something more from you, it is understandable that you resent it. You have already devoted your whole life to them. How could you give them more?

Once you have put them outside yourself—once they are real people, not the people of your imagination—then you can have so much more, so much more for you, and so much more for them.

Giving up your fantasy family means you'll be gaining a real family—real people.

So there is no cause for guilt. You are not rejecting or hurting the feelings of real people—only those you have created in your imagination.

Let us tell you about this young woman who lived alone. But in her fantasy she was keeping house for her daddy. Her father, who lived in another state, became gravely ill. She wouldn't even telephone him. She felt no need to communicate with him, though she couldn't explain it rationally.

Only when she saw how she carried him with her in her fantasy could she actually give him more in reality.

Then she could telephone, express her concern, visit him, and comfort him.

Before that she was constantly giving to him, but *he* never received anything.

THREE

It Takes Two Separate People

OK—so you're not carrying them around with you.

Can you avoid getting pulled into them?

Pulled into them?

Yes.

It is so easy to forget:

What *you* need.

What *you* want.

What *you* care about.

What's important to *you*.

Who *you* are.

Have you ever noticed those times when you're trying to work something out with someone and you get caught up in the other person's point of view?

IF YOU ARE ON THEIR SIDE
AND IF THEY ARE ON THEIR SIDE
WHO IS ON YOUR SIDE?

It's really OK to be on your own side.

If you have yourself for a friend, you have a friend for life.

It doesn't mean you're a bad person. It means your point of view is at least as important to you as another person's.

No matter how you look at it, if there are two people involved, there can be two attitudes.

Don't be afraid to discover a difference.

It makes life interesting.

You'll work it out and all the better.

Why should either of you be taken for granted?

Just to avoid a confrontation?

Just to avoid that feeling of being a separate person?

Go ahead—try it.

It's not so bad to find out that other people have feelings. That you have feelings.

And that the world exists outside your head.

You don't get along better with other people just by learning techniques—such as how to be a good conversationalist and how to be poised and well mannered.

———•———

Have you ever thought what it means to you to get close to another person?

Are you the one whose ideas get lost?

Do you always have to give in?

Are you so big that you are always the understanding one?

If you are constantly threatened with disappearing into the other person's wishes, then of course you have to back away from other people.

Makes sense.

Possibly you have had a lot of bad times with people. It may seem to you that they tend to take advantage, to take you for granted.

Before you give up on people,

Before you give up on closeness,

Before you give up on love,

Consider:

Have you got the courage to take a good hard look at yourself?

Can you at least entertain the possibility that *you* might have something to do with those unhappy outcomes?

It's not easy to admit any such thing.

We're not even asking you to tell us or anyone else.

Take a chance.

This is all between you and yourself.

It wouldn't happen if you didn't let it happen.

So many people seem to convey the invitation:

"My house is your house.

Your wish is my wish."

But implicit in that charming graciousness, in that sweeping gesture of appearing all-giving, is the expectation that the *other person will know how far to go*.

When by your behavior you seem to put yourself so completely at another person's disposal, you implicitly expect that other person to know your needs and to respect your needs.

You expect the other person to know the limitations of *how much you can comfortably give*, how far you can go.

When you say, "My life is your life," you entrust the boundaries and shape and direction of your life to the other person.

You have issued a sweeping invitation to someone else to make free with your life.

You also expect the other person to protect you from your own openness, your own generosity.

But you are really not being generous and kind.

You are setting a trap.

You are setting up a situation in which you will inevitably feel

Abused,

Taken advantage of, and resentful.

When you expect another person to protect you from your own unwillingness to be in charge of what you can give, you are placing an impossible demand on that other person.

Instead of gratitude for all your self-sacrifice, you are much more likely to be rejected.

It is impossible to live with a self-sacrificing saint.

When you give up what you want, just to give in to the other person's needs, then you are not there.

And when you are not there, the other person is lonely.

And needs to look for company.

FOUR

Protect Us
From The Power Of
The Victims

The power of powerless people is remarkable.

They are very good at making other people play the parts they have written for them.

The young woman in the therapy group was complaining bitterly. Every time she was forced to have lunch with her mother, it was a horrible experience.

No matter how hard she tried, her mother was a "bitch" who always got angry and did her best to make her daughter feel rotten.

The young woman was very convincing.

We were all in sympathy with the innocent, well-intentioned daughter.

We could feel her pain as she described being relentlessly picked on and put down by her mother.

But as the group listened and asked questions the picture began to blur and other images emerged.

The mother valued good grooming. It appeared that the daughter made a point of dressing a little more sloppily than usual when she met her mother for lunch.

The daughter managed to be late for their appointments, even though she knew her mother also valued promptness.

It became clear, as she went into the details of the conversation, that the daughter consistently brought up those topics about which the two had long-standing disagreements.

As we listened we began to understand that the daughter baited her mother into losing her temper. That made it possible for the daughter to erupt with her own pent-up anger.

Somehow the group was able to help her see that she was provoking her mother to behave that way. It was not simply that her mother was mean, rotten, and terrible to her. There was some need on the part of the daughter to get her mother to behave in a destructive way.

The group was able to see that for her own reasons it was important to the daughter that the mother "mistreat" her.

She dreaded these lunches precisely because she knew how they had to end. It was a big step for her to be able to see that she really got what she wanted.

A man in the group helped her when he said, "We're all with you and we want you to know that you have a choice. Just as you can make these lunches come out horrid, you also have the power to make them come out much better.

"Just sit there at lunch and remember what *you* want, and half the battle will be over."

In the ensuing weeks it turned out that there was a great deal of truth in what the man said, and "lunch with mother" took on a completely different character for the young woman.

And so another victim discovered her power.

Would you believe that without knowing it one person can control the behavior of another?

Sounds like science fiction?

More science than fiction.

There are a number of demonstrations which show just that.

What is particularly intriguing about the example that follows is that no one but the experimenter knew what was going on. A message was received and behavior changed without either the senders or receivers of the message being aware.

A psychology teacher in a western college told his students that they would earn course credits if they would spend an hour or so of their time talking about anything at all—whatever interested them— with the patients in the Veterans' Administration Hospital down the road.

The same professor then told the V.A. patients that they would be visited by the students and as part of an experiment each V.A. patient was asked to monitor the speech of one undergraduate.

The patient-monitors were told that the object of the experiment would be to count the number of times words with feeling and excitement were used in normal conversation. In order to make the counting easy, the entire conversation of each of the visiting students would be tape-recorded. Each time the visiting student used a word with feeling, the monitoring patient was asked to simply say, "Uh-huh."

These were the only instructions given to the patients.

Nothing at all was added to the instructions to the students except that they were to do a good deed and make conversation with the shut-ins.

When each of the tapes thus produced was analyzed most of them revealed a steady increase in the amount of feeling and excitement recorded in the speech of the students. What had happened was that the attentiveness of the listeners as evidenced by their "uh-huhs" seemed to encourage or reward the speakers whose behavior changed measurably in the rewarded direction.

In another college on the East Coast, a class in social psychology was taught by one of our friends, and our nephew (now Dr. Robert Mendelsohn) happened to be one of the students. We were able to verify the story which follows from both these first-hand sources.

The instructor was detained and missed the opening of class by about ten minutes.

During this time, the students decided to find out if the conditioning techniques which they had been learning really worked.

Our friend the instructor was a "pacer." She had the habit, as she lectured, of walking back and forth in front of the class. She paced from the door to the window and back from the window to the door. The experimentally minded students agreed among themselves in advance that they would react differently depending on the instructor's position in the room. When she was near the door, they would show little or no interest in their teacher. In that position she would be treated to a classroom of students who would look listlessly at the ceiling or at the floor and look bored as they slumped in their seats, stifling yawns. When the unwary instructor moved toward the window, the students agreed they would sit up attentively, lean forward expectantly, look bright-eyed and eager, and raise their hands to ask questions.

The results of this conspiracy were quite predictable. After a short while our friend was rooted to the window. Unaccountably she was no longer pacing. She was quite pleased with the way her lecture was going and had no idea that her freedom of movement had been tampered with.

The students, however, could not contain themselves. They began to laugh and finally broke down and explained their plot.

Whether you know it or not, you are always influencing the behavior of others by your response (or lack of response!).

It is exciting to discover the power that you possess and have been exercising without even knowing it.

It makes a world of difference to use your powers

consciously and constructively, and you will discover that you no longer need to feel like such a victim.

You can take charge of your life.

FIVE

Can You Do It For Yourself?

Can you do it for yourself?

You can get yourself together getting ready for a date.
Can you do it for yourself?

You can get yourself "up" for that important interview.
Can you do it for yourself?

You can get on the stage and play the part.
Can you do it for yourself?

You can speak eloquently for your client.
Can you do it for yourself?

You can do a good job for your boss.
Can you do it for yourself?

You can study for a grade.
Can you do it for yourself?

Our son Bob was down in the dumps, feeling low and sorry for himself. He went to see the campus counselor who recognized him from Bob's daily radio talk show. After a while he said to Bob:

"You can be the sad person you are now or you can be that cheerful and enthusiastic fellow I hear on your show. Why do you save that wonderful guy for your radio audience? Why not be that way all the time?"

Another son of ours, Neal, was usually a reluctant shopper. Consequently I was unprepared for a sudden display of courtly behavior on his part. He held doors open, offered to carry the packages, and even asked if there was anything else he could do to be helpful. I was pleased but puzzled.

"What's going on? Are you feeling all right?"

"Oh, I'm just trying to be mature. Is this mature?"

"It seems so. Now tell me—what's this all about?"

Neal said, "Well, you saw the letter which came yesterday. I can make that special class. But the letter said it's only for those pupils who are psychologically and emotionally mature. And I want to make that class."

Bob has been enthusiastic and Neal has been mature.

Surely you have known at least one young man whose entire bearing, manner, and dress went through a complete transformation because he met the girl of his dreams.

Then there was the man who wanted to come into analysis but had no job.

"You see, my problem is, I can't get or hold a job."

The analyst conceded that this was indeed a serious problem, but on the other hand he would have to work in order to pay for treatment.

The man came back the next week, having gotten a job, and he has not been out of work since.

There's the kid down the block who flunked out of school. Could barely read. And math? Forget it! Now you should see him poring through auto service manuals and calculating engine tolerances to three decimal places.

Really *wanting* makes the difference.

Do you really *want*?

Please stop for a minute right here.

It may seem like a small thing; but if you have been saying—

"I can't"

When you really mean—

"I won't"

Then you've been wasting a lot of sweat, a lot of energy, a lot of effort.

This is one of those crucial points where there is absolutely no substitute for being completely honest with yourself.

It's OK with us if for some reason you have to kick up a lot of sand, make prodigious efforts to show other people how hard you are trying.

But please.

Don't kid *yourself*.

To try hard against your own not wanting is to spin your wheels. It's like driving with the parking brake on.

If you say—

"I want, but I can't"

You are not saying—

"I want"

You are saying—

"I can't want."

You are not allowing yourself to want what you can.

It may be that you have talked yourself into trying to want just those things which will please others.

Forget it.

Your best bet is to know what you want, and go for it.

But to do that,

You have to know

who you are.

That's asking a lot, but you deserve it.

You deserve a life that is tailor-made for you.

You deserve what is yours—uniquely, specially, and personally for you.

There is no way you can have this tailor-made existence unless you know your own dimensions, unless you know just who you are and exactly what you want to be.

SIX

You Can
Take Charge Of
Your Life

We've talked about not kidding yourself.

We've said: level with yourself.

It's clear that being in charge of your life has to rest solidly on knowing who you are and what you really want.

Easier said than done.

Maybe it shouldn't be so difficult.

After all, you've been there the whole time.

How can anyone know you better than you do?

Sounds very logical, but most of us are busy covering up who we really are, just as fast as we can uncover our true selves. It's like trying to dig a cave in a sand hill. The faster you dig the faster it pours in and covers up.

Incidentally, that's what psychoanalysis is all about—helping people get straight with themselves. Not telling them what to be, but helping them to find out who they are, and how to become what they really want to be.

Here are some of the things which can help you to do what the ancients recommended,

"Know Thyself."

Begin by not sitting in judgment on yourself.

Don't get all hung up, for the moment, with whether you think you're good, bad, indifferent.

Don't concern yourself with whether you're better or worse than other people.

Instead, try to know yourself, as the kind of person you are.

Can you say what is important to you in life? If you can answer this right off and honestly, you're off to a head start. You still may have to zero in on it in more indirect ways.

What turns you on? What was it the last time you really felt turned on, enthusiastic, stirred by something? How about the half-dozen times before that?

If you can answer these questions, you've got some powerful clues to your real identity.

If your response is that you almost never feel turned on, if you are working against yourself and depriving yourself, then you are going to have to do some real pick-and-shovel work on yourself. You will have to dig, because you have got yourself wrapped in a blanket of gray gloom that keeps you from letting any sunshine into your life.

When you are free to choose, how do you spend your time? Is there some kind of activity that keeps you interested? Whatever reason you might give yourself for doing it, you might have here an important thread which can help you to unravel the mystery of who you are. On the other hand, if you find yourself in your free time doing nothing but sleeping, daydreaming, watching television, that's a pretty good sign that you are now reading something that you need very much and which can change your life. To be passively involved during most of your leisure time in fantasies—your own or somebody else's—could mean that your life is lacking in real satisfaction. It could mean that the person you would like to be exists mainly in your fantasy and that you are not bringing that self out into the real world.

———•———

You can also pick up some good clues to yourself if you take a look at how you feel about nonleisure time. *What are the things about work (or school) that you like to do? What satisfaction do you get?* It is a measure of your creativity and adaptability to find something interesting, something worth your time and effort in whatever you do. It can be an important source of satisfaction to be the best you can be at whatever you are doing. If you can give yourself the pleasure that comes from doing a job you know is well done, even if the work is not of your choosing, then you've got it made. Alternatively, if the mandatory chores of life represent unrelieved displeasure for you, you have our profound sympathy. There are always things we may not choose to do, but which have to be done. If you just keep telling yourself how awful it is, you make it a double burden. If you have to spend your day breaking hard rocks, can you at least take pleasure in the force and accuracy with which you swing your hammer? If you keep in mind only the resentment you feel at your enforced labor, how can you be sure that there isn't some way to make it easier, quicker, more pleasant for yourself?

If you were completely relieved of the usual practical considerations—if you got that inheritance from the "rich uncle," if all possibilities were open for you—what's the first thing you would do? And then what? What would you do with your life? This question can be fun, because it can help you to make your fantasies conscious. By the way, is there a fantasy that you already know you have, something you keep coming back to?

What do you tend to think of regularly just before you fall asleep?

If you are able to sort of play around lightly with these questions, you might find answers come more readily. Don't be so grim and deadly serious. Many a true word *is* said in jest. Also treat yourself with kindness and respect. Please, please, don't put yourself down if the picture that is emerging is not to your liking. This is one time to really be on your own side and give yourself sympathetic understanding. Respect the life you have been living even though you may want to change it in some way. There were probably very good reasons for you to have turned out this way.

When you can look at yourself and be fair, honestly but not harshly, then it may be possible for you to face some truths. Can you face the fact that you're not an angel? In case you need reminding, neither is anyone else. One of the comforts, if you happen to be a believer, is that we of this earth are only human and there are very few saints among us. And no angels.

Can you face the fact that some of the things you've been telling yourself may not be true?

Can you face the fact that you made a mistake?

Facing the mistakes and misconceptions of your life does not mean emphasizing them or exaggerating them out of all proportions. It is simply a matter of taking the bitter with the better so that you can own the personality which you have created up to now.

Created?

Yes, isn't that wild and wonderful, too. In very important ways you have created yourself whether you know it or not. As you grow up, and as you go through life, you are constantly picking up and adding things to how and who you are. These are little character traits, little mannerisms, a way of talking, a way of walking, a facial expression, a gesture, even ways of thinking and believing, that you have borrowed, imitated, and made your own. It may have been from your parents or others in the household; a favorite teacher; a friend; characters in a book, on the stage, on the screen. Maybe you borrowed from somebody you didn't even like. It may have been from someone who made you feel uncomfortable or afraid. Imitating that person could have been a way of making you feel less afraid, and a way of impressing others.

You've taken these little bits and pieces and blended them into—you! If you've created a unified and harmonious whole, you are the exception. After all, most of it was done when you were quite young and some of the bits and pieces may have come from the strangest places. This process of putting yourself together takes place almost automatically. It is a wonder that so many people do such a good job of it since it occurs almost incidental to growing up.

Doesn't it make good sense at some point in your life to take stock, step back from what you have created? Have a look at it. If need be remodel it, reshape it. This is what any creative person has to do from time to time. If you're painting a picture, making a sculpture, or what-have-you—you also step back, relax, and look at your handiwork from a fresh perspective.

After all, *you are the most important creative activity of your life.*

The process of taking inventory of yourself is something that some people do routinely. Maybe one of the reasons you've kept yourself from doing it is because you've felt a little funny about having been an imitator. Maybe you have felt that because you have been trying to be like so-and-so, you've been playing a part and not really yourself. That's not a very rare hangup, but you don't have to get hung up on it. Nobody, but nobody can create a self from scratch. Everyone has to do the same thing. We happen to live at a time in history when there is more freedom, more to choose from, more possible ways to be than ever before. The way in which you go about choosing, the elements that attract you as the building blocks for your own personality, and the ways in which you put them together spell out that which is uniquely you. Everybody chooses from what's available. Even though you may have clothed yourself in borrowed finery, you are not a fraud. After all, who has been doing the choosing? You can be sure that no one else has ever put together exactly the same combinations that you have. Don't forget, there are only twelve notes in a musical scale, and yet many hundreds of thousands of unique and beautiful compositions have been created. It's all a question of how they are put together. It doesn't make you any less to have taken from others.

The wonderful thing to understand—what comes to so many as a stunner, a shocker—is that you do not have to take yourself as a prepackaged product coming off the assembly line. There are certain things you have inherited—your coloring, your sex, your bone structure, your height—but what you do with your biological inheritance is up to you. *Much of what you are you have made*, and it is your right, if not also your obligation, to remake yourself exactly as you see fit.

And why shouldn't you do a better job of it, now?

You've had a lot more experience since you first started putting yourself together. You know a lot more about what works and what doesn't work for you.

If you see something you don't like, the chances are *you* put it there, and *you* can change it.

SEVEN

Introduce Yourself To You

We know someone who has grown up to be
quite a guy. When he was younger, he would an-
nounce:

"I'm the kind of kid who has to roller-skate,
I'm the kind of kid who needs to play ball.
I'm the kind of kid who likes to take showers,
     not baths."

This kind of self-affirmation, this kind of talking
to yourself and to those around you, builds that
important self-image, that important self-concept,
without which it is impossible to take charge of
your life.

Parents can be of great help by defining the child
to himself.

A parent may say:

"You like to do things with your hands."

This reflects back to the child a self-image and also helps to start the very habit of self-definition.

Unfortunately too many people tell themselves who they are only when they are being uncomplimentary.

To describe yourself, to fill in the picture of the kind of person you are, fulfills the need everyone has for a reasonably reliable and objective self-evaluation. There is no point in telling yourself you can run a four-minute mile if that's not who you are. There is no point in giving yourself a self-description that is too removed from reality.

Nor do you do yourself any kindness if you underestimate who you are. And most people underestimate who they can be. Sure enough it is difficult to be realistic about yourself in certain respects. But instead of getting hung up with the difficult ones there are many simple truths about each one of us that are easy to get at.

What's your favorite color?

What's your favorite food?

What's your favorite car?

What's your favorite kind of furniture?

What kind of clothing do you prefer?

Do you like the city or the country?

What season do you prefer?

Do you like to read?

What kind of books?

Do you like music?

What kind of music do you like?

Do you like to watch TV?

What are your favorite programs?

How do you sleep?

   on your back?

   on your stomach?

   on your side?

If the answers to these questions have been popping into your mind quite readily, that's very encouraging. You are more likely to be a well-defined personality, with clearcut tastes and preferences.

Have you been saying "I don't know" to these questions about likes and dislikes?

Many people are likely to give that kind of response. And that is rather sad.

The reasons for the "I don't know" response could be:

You're a sorehead.

71

You don't want to give anyone the satisfaction of knowing that you like anything or enjoy anything. That's your privilege, but don't get carried away with your act. Even if no one else is let in on it, it's all right for *you* to know what you like. The chances are, if you are a professional sorehead, you're holding out for something. *Don't you think you should know what you want? Otherwise how will you ever know when you get it?* And how will you know when it's time to stop being sore? You can get stuck in that rut for life.

Or maybe, the reason you "don't know" is: *You've got something to hide.*

You're right, of course. If you let people know what you want and what you like, then they can get a pretty fair notion of who you are. And maybe you have good reason for not trusting others with the "low-down" about yourself. But don't forget this is still all between you and yourself, and why hide from yourself? It's not so bad to admit who you are. If you still don't like it when it's right out there for you to see, then you can do something about it.

But if you close your eyes to it, it's still there.

You may be afraid of finding out that you are not as much as you would like to be. If this is your reason for keeping yourself vague and undefined— please remember this: the only way you can become more is by adding to what you already are.

———•———

To many people, admitting what they want to do *now* is like admitting *everything* they ever wanted. So that, if you are presently ambitious, it is as if you would be broadcasting that you wanted to be first when you were little.

Then, it wasn't your turn.

Because you couldn't have grown-up things when you were little doesn't mean you can't let yourself have them now. You can let yourself know that you want them, now. Now it is your turn. Your time is now.

It may be hard to believe, but there are some big blank empty spaces in your personality.

Being in charge of your life is especially difficult because you haven't given yourself much to be in charge of. We're going to try, as we go along, to help you find ways of filling out your personality and filling in the blank spaces.

It's really not as difficult as it may seem to fill yourself in. The truth is everyone has likes and dislikes, tastes, judgments, attitudes, prejudices, and values.

You simply have not taken the time or the trouble to put yourself to the task of articulating and defining them.

It just helps to say clearly to yourself (doesn't matter if you move your lips or not) what you like. That's all we're talking about. Just fill in your own blank spaces.

I like ——————————————————————

I enjoy doing ————————————————————

It's even a good exercise to imagine what it would be like if you were newborn this very moment with no past and no history.

What would you like to like?

What kind of person would you like to be, given a fresh start?

We hope you'll take a little time and think about this one or at least make a note to come back to this page if you're reading through for the first time. There may be other places as you read along where you might want to do the same thing.

But before you move on, jot down the first thoughts you had in response to what you read.

Only if you want to.

It's up to you.

If you still feel somewhat stuck about knowing who you are and taking charge of the big things in your life, there are a number of things you can do to get yourself going.

Try making small decisions.

Try taking charge in small ways. Make your decision to take charge ahead of time, so that you know it's your decision. Don't wait for someone to make a suggestion first. You may then feel that the only way you can be sure it's your decision is to do the opposite. That's a trap. To have to be opposite is not to be free. If you have to say "white" every time somebody else says "black," and if you have to say "black" every time somebody else says "white," then you're a push-over. Anybody can make you do what they want.

Decide in advance about something small, like

what you want for breakfast or what you're going to wear in the morning. . . . Just a little decision like that, taken consciously and in advance can give you strength. You are developing *the habit of being decisive*, an important part of being in charge of your life.

And remember—you are that person who decided what to eat for breakfast and what to wear that morning.

And feel good about that. Feel good about the fact that you're getting to know what you want, what you like, and that you're not going to go through a lifetime of waiting for someone else to tell you.

Here's another hint for getting to know what you want.

You probably are so completely out of the habit of thinking of yourself in an active way, that when you ask yourself those "What do I like" and "What do I want" questions, you're likely to draw a blank.

If you put it to yourself this way, it might come out differently:

If you ask, "What would I like to see happen?" it might be easier.

Put this way, you're just sitting there without

taking any particular responsibility. If you can get some answers, then you may more readily tune in on your own desires and wishes. Then it's not such a big step from what you would like to see happen to what you want. This in turn can prepare the way for the big one, which is:

"What can *I* do to *make* it happen?"

By the way, here's a small but important consideration. It is possible that you have been keeping yourself from knowing what you like and want because it seems that to have the thought, you've got to do the deed. You know we're not advocating inactivity, but there's a certain benefit which comes from allowing yourself to think anything you want and then taking your time before deciding what to do.

Impulsive action doesn't add to your strength. Strength comes from *really knowing* what you want, and deciding.

Remember, there is a distinction between thinking and doing.

———•———

As you tune in on yourself, make a special effort to catch the ideas, the thoughts, the feelings that flash into your mind just briefly. These flashes may prove to be the keys to the important things that are really you.

It is as if you have gotten into the lifelong habit of putting yourself down so consistently that if an idea is your own, you tend to dismiss it.

You may believe, without knowing it, that the only things worthwhile are things you've heard somewhere or read somewhere.

You don't give yourself a chance to be uniquely and originally yourself.

It all relates to trusting yourself. If you learn to trust yourself, you won't push down a thought that seems crazy or odd. That's the way original thinking has to appear, at first.

Take a chance and turn the new idea over in your mind. Play with it. You may find it fascinating.

Out of a little idea can come the most meaningful and important things in your entire life.

When you listen to your feelings, then you have yourself.

You may be afraid that you are being self-indulgent if you listen to your own thoughts.

It is not self-indulgent to entertain your own thoughts, because only then do you really have enough of yourself to give to others. Otherwise you are simply reflecting what you admire in others back to them.

Don't be afraid that if you really give of what is genuinely and essentially you, you will be depleted.

Quite the contrary. Once you have learned how to tune in on your inner self, you will have tapped a well that never runs dry.

EIGHT

How You Feel About Yourself Throughout The Day Is Life Itself

As you acquire the habit of being in touch with yourself, of being together with yourself, you may be in for a bit of a surprise. There is more in you than just thoughts.

You are full of feelings.

What you feel is at least as important as what you think.

How do you feel when you get out of bed in the morning?

Do you drag yourself out?

Or do you bounce onto your feet full of enthusiasm for the new day?

Your particular response reveals a great deal about how you feel about life.

Pay attention to all your reactions throughout the day.

It is a never-ending source of delight and wonderment to observe what happens when people "have" their feelings.

It is true that in order to have your good feelings you're taking a chance at becoming aware of your painful ones. At some time in your life you might have promised yourself that those painful feelings are just too hard to take and you'd just rather not have any feelings. If so, you made a bad bargain. In order to save yourself some pain, you've practically deprived yourself of the feeling of being alive.

It's how you feel about yourself throughout the day that gives the tone, the texture, and the quality to life itself.

So, tune in on your feelings, and be prepared to make some fascinating discoveries, as well as to feel more alive.

We've known many people who've discovered the strangest feelings. For example, they found that they believed they couldn't have both successful careers and happy personal lives. With some people this may be a clearly defined thought, but there are many more who do not realize that they have this vague sense of having to do some kind of mental balancing act. For some reason it's never two good things that are thus balanced. It's an irrational feeling of having to pay off something good with something bad—like "lucky in cards, un-lucky in love."

When you're in touch with the feeling, it's easier to see that it's nonsense. You do not have to balance the good with the bad.

Do you have a personal superstition that holds you back?

The private myths that are part of feeling depressed get in the way of taking charge.

Do you have a sense of helplessness?

Do you feel hopeless?

Are you embittered?

Do you doubt that you're worth much?

Are you always to blame?

The failures and disappointments of the past do not have to cloud your expectations of today and tomorrow.

The past should not be used to prejudice you against yourself and make you superstitiously fearful about life.

Such feelings only serve to guarantee additional failures and disappointments.

You cannot take charge of the present if you are busy reliving the failures of the past.

Have the courage to confront and deal with your negative feelings.

It's not easy, but don't let the difficulty of all this deter you from the real job of filling in the picture of who you are and what you want for yourself.

NINE

Play Your Own Character

———•———

Here is an example of a person who had no point of view, and the story of how he was helped to become himself.

He was a talented television character actor who could play any part. But off camera he could not be himself.

I said to him in the first session:

"I bet you can't even do a very simple arithmetic problem."

He said:

"Absolutely. You're absolutely right. I don't know any arithmetic. I can't understand it at all."

It became clear to me that he had a great need not to understand, not to make connections, not to know what he liked, not to know who he was.

This is what he had to have an analyst for— I was not his first analyst—to tell him who he was.

When I told him that I was going to help him find out who he was, he laughed. For eight years of treatment with different analysts no one had ever suggested that it could be done. He had somehow accepted the fact that no one could help him in this respect.

It is true that some people wait to be defined, but he had to be redefined every day.

This man could never understand any intellectual concepts, though it was clear that he was not at all lacking in intelligence. If he were not basically intelligent it would not have been possible for him to have played so many roles so brilliantly. But to hear him speak, it was easy to see how he blocked himself from using his mind.

He would not only say—

"I don't understand it"

He also said—

"I never will understand it."

It was suggested that what he should do was to play "himself."

What I said was:

"If I were you, I would play the character of myself. I would approach this as I would approach preparing myself for any characterization. I would attempt to understand the motivation of the character. I would study his background, where he came from, where he's going, what he's doing in the present."

He liked the idea of approaching himself as he would a character in a script. Somehow this was less frightening to him and therefore made it more possible.

Of course, we also spent time discussing why he had been unwilling to play the character of himself —what he was afraid of and what he needed to hide.

I told him that he reminded me of a girl I had known who would never allow herself to think. At first it had been that she would never allow herself to think in the presence of her parents. Later on it became too frightening for her to have thoughts in the presence of any others. It was possible to trace her fear back to a time when she was less than three years old. It seems that she had just discovered the pleasures of playing with her own body. Delighted with her discovery, she babbled happily to her parents. Unfortunately the parents were rather straightlaced and completely unprepared to deal with their daughter's discovery. Because of their own early training, no doubt, and their own fears, they reacted with horror and outrage and beat her severely.

As I told this story he had his first comprehending reaction in my office and he said:

"I can understand that. I could believe something like that happened to me. Do you think that something like that happened to me? I have no memory of it."

I responded with:

"I don't know if something like that did happen to you, maybe yes, maybe no, and maybe even if it did happen we will not get to it, but perhaps we can go on the assumption that it did, since this story seems to mean so much to you. Then perhaps what we can do is just go back and fill in the different things you do remember in your early life, and we can start with any age you want."

Once he got the idea of building his character and once he could understand what he had been avoiding in not playing it, in not being it, he could begin to fill in the specifics of who this character was. He could understand something about himself at different ages of his life.

He began to remember the kinds of games he liked to play as a child. He recalled his favorite sports, his favorite stories, his favorite songs. Then he could remember, as he got into his teens, how he became increasingly dependent on his older sister for guidance in matters of taste and preference. Over the years this dependency passed on to teachers, directors, girlfriends, finally his wife, and of course his series of analysts.

By means of reconstructing his early life, he got to the point where he was increasingly in charge of himself.

As he began to fill himself in, to fill in the picture of who he was, he no longer had to be redefined every day. He could really catch hold, at first only for as long as a session, then maybe until the next session or the next two sessions and then for a week or two, and then hopefully forever.

An amazing thing happened. He became a real presence in my office. At first the room had seemed to contain only my presence and this other figure. In those early sessions with him I found that I was having ten times as much feeling as with anyone else. I would have to feel for the two of us. It was a most extraordinary experience for me—as if there was no other person in the room with me, hardly a flicker. Usually I have a sense of myself and another person.

It was a relief for me and a source of gratification to both of us to find him increasingly becoming a definite presence in the room. This occurred as he acquired his own point of view, as he could express his own feelings and make known his own wishes.

What this man was finding out about himself was that he had been keeping himself this vague person. He had thought that was all there was to him. In order to feel safe he had managed to convince himself that he was empty inside. In this way he did not have to feel afraid of exposure.

We never did find out any specific incident which may have marked the beginning of his pattern of hiding, but the story I had told him about that little girl released him from the desperate need to cover up.

Gradually he was able to understand more and more for himself.

He would come in and say:

"I can even understand other people's thoughts now."

"I can understand the concept of gravity."

In time he experienced that release of energy that comes about from not holding on so tightly to the need not to know. That energy can then be used to know.

And one day he said:

"You know, the strength you take to live unhappily, if you take just half of that and put it into living well, you can have a pretty good time."

TEN

Getting Into
Action

Getting started is the hardest thing.

It's the law of inertia.

An object at rest takes a much greater amount of energy to move than when it is already rolling.

For this reason you often hear this advice to someone who seems stuck.

"Make any decision, any move, even if it's the wrong one. It's better than just sitting there."

We would agree.

But action which is based on knowing who you are is of course much better than just striking out randomly for the sake of getting going.

If you know what your values are—

If you know what your standards are—

If you know what is important to you—

If you have a point of view—

Then you have a sense of direction.

Then you know where you are going.

Then something has relevance or lacks relevance to a particular personal goal.

Knowing yourself, you can see if it moves you toward what you want or away from it.

If you don't know what's important to you, you are much more likely to have trouble getting started.

Without knowing it, you may be waiting for someone to tell you what to do.

Make a habit of checking yourself to be sure that the things you do are actually and affirmatively of your own choosing. It is so easy to slide along in old habits of doing what others expect and decide for you.

The only way to break an old habit is to start a new one.

Even here you have a choice.

You are in charge of which habit you will want to strengthen.

It's up to you.

Please remember, however, that just because *your* choice may coincide with someone else's, it does not mean that it's not *your* choice.

You have seen how making a decision says something about you. It is also true that not making a decision says something about you.

Here again it's up to you.

Is there any really good reason why you should not stand up for the kind of person you are?

If you know who you are, your choices are made easier since you are less likely to be in conflict with different parts of yourself.

Don't get hung up on the end of a pendulum, swinging back and forth between *"yes"* and *"no."*

Giving yourself such a conflict probably means that you are avoiding facing something about who you are.

Like any obsession, excessive conflict is a cover-up. The *"yes"* and *"no"* of the conflict is a distraction to keep you preoccupied so that you do not pay attention to something else.

If you don't know what you're feeling, you lose control of your feelings and your body might have to express those feelings for you. So instead of giving yourself a conflict you may be giving yourself a psychosomatic symptom, such as headaches, hives, allergies, asthma, ulcers.

The same may be true of excessive anxiety. You can spook yourself into not being and not knowing all of what you are.

Keep in mind,

Your anxiety is part of you.

It's not bigger than you are.

It is only one of your feelings.

You have many feelings and you are bigger than any one of them.

The first twinge of anxiety is a tipoff for you to pay attention. It's a signal.

Don't run away from it. This is the feeling you may be most tempted to ignore or evade.

After all, anxiety can be uncomfortable, so we can understand the temptation to pretend you're not feeling it.

Besides, you've always been told not to be scared. So it's unseemly.

But you can never be more grown-up than when you can look your anxiety in the eye and take charge of it.

When you stop running away from it, stand your ground, and face it, it has a way of shrinking to manageable size.

Now is the time to use your courage.

When you catch your anxiety when it is small, it is much, much easier to deal with. (The same thing is true of depression. Get it early before it snowballs into a big cloud of gloom.)

You are much more likely to trip over the anxiety which you have shoved under the rug.

At this early stage, you are in a position to make your anxiety work for you rather than against you.

Carol Channing, the Broadway star, says:

"Tension can be an asset, if you make it work for you. It keeps you on your toes."

Arnold Palmer, the champion golfer, says he prefers being "a bit keyed-up" before a tournament because "the extra adrenaline helps you play better."

What these stars have discovered is something that everyone can have going for him.

There is a fine line between anxiety and excitement.

If you do not let anxiety stop you, you can nudge it over the line into excitement and give yourself a fine competitive edge.

But don't wait for anxiety to turn into panic. Then your feeling is controlling you instead of vice versa.

Be the rider, not the horse.

Kierkegaard, the nineteenth-century Danish philosopher, first described what has come to be known as "threshold anxiety." He describes the feelings of a young man who is about to leave home to go out into the world to seek his fortune. As he stands on the threshold of the house, about to leave, he feels that he's turning his back on everything that is warm, familiar, and secure—what he has known all his life. Beyond the threshold lies the world, filled with all that is unknown and strange. If the young man turns back at this point, he is lost. If, however, he can take the fear of the unknown and turn it into the excitement of the unlimited possibilities which are open before him, he grows in the moment and is alive, as never before.

If you have the courage to welcome your anxiety instead of having to retreat at the first twinge, you will be rewarded. The chances are you are on the threshold of growth. It can be a signal of new adventures, new possibilities in your life.

We heard of a wonderful man who left school at an early age to help support his family. Now at the age of forty, he has done quite well in providing for himself and those who depended on him. He confessed to a friend that he had always wanted to be a physician but he was afraid that he was now too old.

"After all," he said, "in four years I'll be forty-four."

And wisely his friend said, "If you don't go to medical school, in four years you'll be forty-four anyway."

Any new venture can mean growth in your abilities and potential. Don't let your anxiety stop you. Use it for yourself.

Anxiety is only one of the ways in which you can stop yourself from being the kind of person who is in charge of your own life. You may also try to convince yourself that there is something about being an active, take-charge person that is distasteful to you.

Some people do seem to need to take charge not only of their own lives but of everything and everyone in sight.

We are trying to help you to take charge of your life, not the whole world.

Our concept of being in charge is based on self-knowledge, self-appreciation, and self-respect, which is more likely to go together with respect and appreciation of others.

The more you feel in charge of your life, the less need you have to control others. The dictatorial ones feel that they are fighting valiantly against overwhelming and crushing odds.

A truly strong person is strong enough to let other people be who they are, and doesn't feel pushed around by the strength of others. A person who feels strong is much more likely to be mild-mannered and easygoing, with an air of quiet confidence.

The specter you may be using to stop yourself, the fear of becoming the hard-driving insensitive activist, is probably illusory.

If you have picked up this book and read this far into it, it is an extremely remote possibility that you are in any danger of turning into an obsessively driven compulsive.

Life has its rhythms, and there is a time for doing and another time for just being. The natural rhythm of things alternates between activity and contemplation. Where there is an excess of passivity, we find it necessary to stress decisiveness and action. But we by no means intend this at the expense of reflectiveness and quiet.

It has been our experience that many people

are too hard on themselves when they should be easy, and too easy on themselves when they should be hard. The only way we know to avoid these pitfalls is to know yourself well.

ELEVEN

How To Get Lucky

When you were small, you could expect that "they" would take care of you and make everything all right.

Being human, they probably "failed" you, and being human, you may still be waiting for them to make good.

Can you do it for yourself?

What? In this day of big government, big business, and a complex society, *do it yourself?*

All the more reason in today's world to speak as a self-respecting adult to your government, your firm, your union. The strategies left over from childhood are not much use now. No one will be moved out of pity for your helplessness, or by your pouting, and surely not by however cute, docile, and dependent you may be. Quite the contrary; if you abdicate your adulthood, it encourages those who are ready to take charge of your life for you.

Taking charge of your life cannot be done for you. It is a right that only you can take for yourself.

To do so means giving up the hidden payoffs, the mythical benefits of not being in charge, the false security that you will always be loved and never lonely and afraid.

To be in charge of your life means leveling with yourself. You have a great deal to do with where you are in life, you gave your parents and society lots of help. Actively or passively, you have allowed things to work out as they have. You have had options and choices you didn't know existed, or that you simply passed up. You still have choices open to you, if you are willing to give up the feeling of being a helpless victim.

Your sense of self—call it self-respect, self-esteem, ego strength, liking and appreciating yourself, being your own best friend—this is the backbone, the central support for being in charge of your life.

Your sense of self is what you have sacrificed in not being in charge. So it is your sense of self that you most urgently need to safeguard. It has to be the most precious part of you. Without it you are not much good to yourself or anyone else. At first, it is a gift of parental love. Soon it becomes something like breathing, which you can only do for yourself.

So take a look at yourself, and see that you have a person there.

Define yourself. Describe yourself. Take a stand. Let yourself know who you are. Then when you know who you are and what you stand for, don't let anything or anyone persuade you to go against yourself. You can never feel good about yourself if you do.

Begin with small decisions, small assertions. Don't bite off so much that you become discouraged. If at times it seems difficult, remember, you are only pitted against your own stubbornness. When you are on your own side, you will have the strength to take on the ills of the world.

May we give you a final word of encouragement? We are not mystics, and we don't deal in magic. But we have seen over and over again something that looks like magic. Once you get on your own side, once you decide to act in your own behalf, you begin to see possibilities and potentials that you never knew were there. It's not mystical. Having learned how to deal with your anxiety and doubts, you are free to see new and challenging things. You have the courage to use the strength and creativity you barely suspected you had. This openness to opportunities and possibilities that others may not see is what often goes under the name of "getting lucky."

William H. Murray put it as beautifully and effectively as we have ever seen, when he said:

"Until one is committed, there is hesitancy, the chance to draw back, always ineffectiveness. Concerning all acts of initiative (and creation), there is one elementary truth, the ignorance of which kills countless ideas and splendid plans: that the moment one definitely commits oneself, then Providence moves too. All sorts of things occur to help one that would never otherwise have occurred. A whole stream of events issues from the decision, raising in one's favor all manner of unforeseen incidents and meetings and material assistance, which no man could have dreamed would have come his way."

Murray concludes, as do we, with this poem of Goethe:

"Whatever you can do, or dream you can, begin it.

Boldness has genius, power and magic in it."

Begin it, now.

ABOUT THE AUTHORS

MILDRED NEWMAN and BERNARD BERKOWITZ, often described as America's best-loved psychologists, are two warm, sensitive people who have been able to make life fulfilling for themselves—and for many, many others.

Their lives are united in marriage and work. Sometimes they speak with one voice. One journalist has remarked that either one can begin a sentence that the other may complete.

And yet they are different. Mildred has been described as fire, Bernie as ice. She is warm, animated; he is cool, thoughtful.

Paradoxically, she comes to analysis by way of Freudian orthodoxy which, in its classical form, is represented by the silent analyst, sitting behind the couch. Bernie's early work was Adlerian, a therapeutic style which is folksy, egalitarian, give and take. Between them, they have evolved a way of helping people deal with their lives.

Their philosophy encourages self-identification and self-fulfillment as an important step toward becoming a total, giving human being. Mildred explains it this way: "If you have deep respect for yourself, you will have respect for others. You will not become self-centered or selfish. You will find yourself increasingly kind, loving and comforting to the people you care about."

Millions of people have responded positively to their books because Mildred and Bernie have been able to distill the approach and the psychoanalytic insights that have proved so successful in their private practice.

"We try to write," says Bernie, "as though the reader was right there in our office." Adds Mildred, "We feel that our books should be an emotional experience, that they can be picked up at different times in a reader's life and that they will be both energizing and comforting in times of crisis."

Their first book, *How To Be Your Own Best Friend*, was originally published privately and later went on to become a 3-million-copy bestseller; *How To Be Awake and Alive* followed in 1975, and the hardcover edition of *How To Take Charge of Your Life* appeared in 1977.

How To Take Charge of Your Life tells how you can transform anxiety into energy and how your capacity for decisiveness can be strengthened. Demystified and free of jargon, the book shows that you are the most important creative activity in your life.

"The truth is," says Mildred, "that all wise, deep things are very simple. This is a book of commonsense. This is a book which is intended to encourage you, provoke you, if necessary, to be you."

These two gifted people can help you find the courage to live the life which is your very own. "If you have but one life to live," they emphasize, "make it the one you choose."

Mildred Newman and Bernard Berkowitz are both native New Yorkers. They first met as teenagers while taking music lessons at Carnegie Hall, only to remeet and marry later on.

Mildred Newman graduated from Hunter College High School and from Hunter College where she received an M.A. in psychology. She completed the analytic training program at the National Psychology Association for Psychoanalysis.

Bernard Berkowitz graduated from the City College of New York, received an M.S. from Columbia University and his doctorate from New York University. He attended the Alfred Adler Institute and the Post Graduate Center for Mental Health. He has been affiliated with the City College of the City University of New York and has had numerous articles and reviews published in professional journals.

Married for fifteen years, each has two children by a previous marriage. Mildred's son and daughter, respectively, are a psychologist and a sociologist. Bernie has two sons: one is a Senate correspondent for Associated Press radio, and the other, a systems analyst with an engineering firm. They have just become grandparents for the third time.

We Deliver!
And So Do These Bestsellers.

Bantam
On Psychology

SPECIAL
MONEY SAVING
OFFER

Now you can have an up-to-date listing of Bantam's hundreds of titles plus take advantage of our unique and exciting bonus book offer. A special offer which gives you the opportunity to purchase a Bantam book for only 50¢. Here's how!

By ordering any five books at the regular price per order, you can also choose any other single book listed (up to a $4.95 value) for just 50¢. Some restrictions do apply, but for further details why not send for Bantam's listing of titles today!

Just send us your name and address plus 50¢ to defray the postage and handling costs.